MiM Mini Guide No.2:

L.C.C. & G.L.C. Selected Projects 1946-1986

Joshua Abbott

MiM Mini Guide No.2: L.C.C. & G.L.C. Selected Projects 1946-1986

Published in the United Kingdom 2022 by Mod in Metro Publishing

www.modernism-in-metroland.co.uk

Words, Photographs and Design by Joshua Abbott

Printed by Mixam Ltd, Watford

Joshua Abbott is hereby identified as the author of this work in accordance with section 77 of the Copyrights, Designs and Patents Acts 1988.

A CIP Catalogue record is available for this book from the British Library.

ISBN: 978-1-7396857-0-6

Our first Mini Guide covered the small but charming houses of the 1930s Frinton Park estate in Essex. Our second guide covers a larger area in time and space, with a selection of non-housing buildings by the London County Council and Greater London Council. We have chosen to focus away from the estates created by these two bodies, instead looking at the schools, fire stations, concert halls, workshops and various other structures built between 1946-86. The estates of the L.C.C. and G.L.C. have gradually been redeveloped and demolished over the last 30 years as society ills have been projected onto them, and they have come to symbolise the blankness of the postwar era. Of course a counter current has rehabilitated the aims and designs of these schemes, but many have been erased from London's landscape already.

From 1946 to 1986, the L.C.C. and G.L.C. built an astounding variety of buildings. Apart from housing estates, the architects departments also designed and built the following; Schools (Primary, Secondary, Special), Colleges, Polytechnics, Teaching Colleges, Concert Halls, Art Galleries, Bowls Clubs, Recreation Centres, Libraries, Fire Stations, Ambulance Stations, Magistrates Courts, Youth Clubs, Community Centres, Workshops, Ventilation Towers, Roads, Bridges, Pumping Stations, Sewage Works, Waste Centres, Flood Defences and much else.

This guide explores some of aforementioned projects, many by now-famous designers. The buildings are arranged in approximate chronological order, with photographs and/or text overviews of each building. Where possible we have included the names of the architects involved with each project including the team leader, job architect and assistants. Because of the large area the guide covers we have not included a map, but all the buildings featured should be easy to find online. Some of the buildings in the guide may have been redeveloped or demolished by the time you read this, but we hope the book is a reminder of the aims and ideals behind them.

The L.C.C. and G.L.C: A Short History 1946-1986

The Luftwaffe bombing campaign that began in 1940, and went on until 1945 through the use of rockets, left London a shattered city. Nearly 30,000 civilians were killed in the capital, with an estimated 1.2 million homes also damaged or destroyed. The London County Council had been formed in 1889, and the architects and planning department had built large estates all over London in the early 20th century, to contend with the growing population. But the devastated city and the postwar consensus gave the L.C.C. the impetus to implement a wide ranging change in the fabric of the capital. Robert Hogg Matthew became the council's Chief Architect in 1946, and with his assistant John Leslie Martin, he set about reconstructing the city.

Aside from replacing damaged housing stock, the L.C.C. architect's department's first task was to plan and design the Festival of Britain, a national show of progress held on the south bank of the Thames in 1951. The centrepiece was the Festival Hall, the ceremonial hub of the festival, and a showcase for Scandinavian inspired postwar modernism. Matthew left in 1953 to go into private practice, with Martin taking over until 1956 when he left to teach at Cambridge. Hubert Bennett assumed the leadership of the architect's department, and continued with the near autonomous sub divisions responsible for Housing, Schools and General Works. Each division was run by a head of department, with hand picked groups of young architects making up the design teams.

This organisation and the scores of young architects in the department led to a battle of styles, as the Scandinavian influenced group contended with the more Corbusier-inspired youngsters. This clash was most stark at the Alton Estate in Roehampton, with its polite Festival-style east side, and more aggressively brutalist west side. This early part of Bennett's tenure was the department's high point, with hundreds of buildings being designed by architects that would go to greater fame in later years. Terry Farrell, Rodney Gordon, John Killick, Stanley Amis, Bill Howell, John Partridge, Ron Herron, Warren Chalk and many others got their start in architectural life with the L.C.C. Many already famous architects were also given commissions to help the department cope with the scale of rebuilding. Erno Goldfinger, Denys Lasdun, Chamberlin, Powell & Bon and Yorke, Rosenberg & Mardall are a few that benefited from the excess of work in the L.C.C. 's in-tray.

The reorganisation of the London County Council into the Greater London Council in 1965, took away much of the architect's departments planning influence, leaving it in charge of large scale housing projects and infrastructure works. Bennett left in 1970, with Roger Walters taking over overall responsibility for projects such as the Thamesmead housing estate. The tide had turned by 1978 when Walters left and the role was taken up by Fred Pooley. Large multi storey projects in concrete were seen as expensive and ugly, with smaller scale buildings consisting of brick, timber and tile, often with pitched roofs, in vogue. The department still managed to produce monumental works such as the Thames Barrier, but the tide was running out.

The Labour-led council's clashes with the Conservative government of Margaret Thatcher led to the Local Government Act of 1985, abolishing the G.L.C. with its powers devolved to the 32 London boroughs. The legacy of the architects department of the G.L.C. and its predecessor can still be seen all over the capital, despite the incessant wrecking ball of the developers. Many of the department's buildings have been listed, especially the non-housing works gathered in this guide. The housing works have fared badly in comparison with constant redevelopment and demolition threatening all but a handful of listed estates.

Chief Architects of the London County Council Architect's Department and Greater London Council Department of Architecture and Civic Design 1946-1986: Robert H. Matthew (1946-53), J. Leslie Martin (1953-6), Hubert Bennett (1956-71), Roger Walters (1971-78), F.B. Pooley (1978-80), P.E. Jones (1980-86)

Housing Group Leaders: H.J. Whitfield Lewis (1950-9), K.J. Campbell (1959-74), G.H. Wrigglesworth (1974-80)

Education Group Leaders: S. Howard (1950-5), M.C.L. Powell (1956-71), G.H. Wrigglesworth (1972-74), P.E. Jones (1974-80)

Special Works Group Leaders: Geoffrey Horsfall (1960-76), R.A. Michelmore (1977-80)

Royal Festival Hall, Southbank
1949-51
London County Council Architect's Department
Robert Mathew, Leslie Martin, Edwin Williams, Peter Moro,
Trevor Dannatt

Alterations & Additions
1962-63
London County Council Architect's Department
Norman Engleback, David Wisdom, Harty Abbot,
Tony Booth, Robert Maxwell

The 1951 Festival of Britain was intended as a tonic for the nation and a showcase for the country's design and technology after the privations of war. A site on the South Bank of the Thames was used as the grounds for the festival, featuring architectural wonders such as the Skylon by Powell & Moya, and the Dome of Discovery by Ralph Tubbs. The Festival Hall was designed as the centerpiece of the site, combining ceremonial and leisure activities.

It was designed by a team of architects from the L.C.C. Architect's Department, led by chief architect Robert Mathew, with Leslie Martin, Peter Moro and Edwin Williams. Others such as designers Robin & Lucienne Day and acoustic specialist Hope Bagenal leant their expertise to the project. The building was constructed of reinforced concrete, with large expanses of glass with wood and limestone used for the interior.

The auditorium was arranged within the structure with plenty of public spaces around it. This insulates the auditorium against traffic sounds from the neighbouring railway bridge. The public spaces were designed to be wide and open, allowing free circulation of patrons, with no separate foyers for different fees.

The building was altered only 13 years after it opened, by the next generation of L.C.C. architects, led by Norman Engleback. They added foyers and terraces overlooking the river, installed additional dressing rooms and added a Portland stone finish to the building, changing the buildings demeanor from the Scandinavin inspired modernism of the original towards a sparer, tougher look more in keeping with the mid 60s. The Festival Hall became the first post war building to receive Grade I listing in 1981 and was renovated in 2007 by Allies and Morrison.

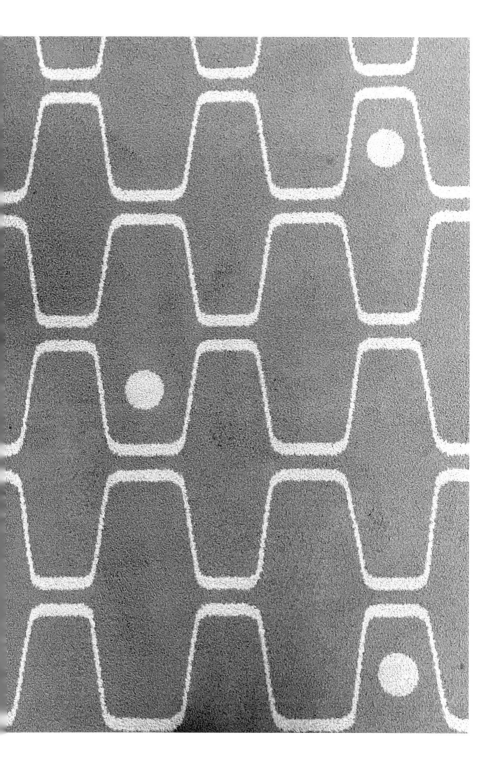

**Brandlehow School, Putney
1950
Erno Goldfinger**

The immediate postwar years saw the need for a mass school building programme, replacing buildings damaged during the war and providing more informal, light-filled schools. To the north of the capital, Hertfordshire County Council had started using prefabricated school designs from 1946. The architect Erno Goldfinger devised his own school building system during World War II. The only fruits of the system are these two primary schools, *Brandlehow* and *Westville Road*, built in the early 1950s (Goldfinger would also design a secondary school, *Haggerston School* in Hackney) Both schools are largely single storey, with fully glazed double height assembly halls. The low profiles of the school buildings are balanced by a tall brick entrance tower containing water tanks. Westville Road (now called Greenside) also features a mural by Gordon Cullen in the entrance hall.

There were a number of other significant L.C.C. primary schools of the time. *Phoenix School* on Bow Road was opened as a special school in 1952. It was designed by Farquharson and McMorran, in the prevailing Festival style, with stock brick and green copper roofs. *Susan Lawrence* and *Elizabeth Lansbury* schools were both built as part of the Live Architecture section of the Festival of Britain in Poplar. Designed by Yorke, Rosenberg & Mardall, they used prefab concrete planes around a steel frame, and decorative tilework by Peggy Angus. *Woodberry Down Primary* (1951) is one of the last surviving parts of the Woodberry Down estate, which also included a secondary school. The primary school was designed by Joseph Berger of the L.C.C. Architect's Department in a sparse, Scandinavian style with yellow stock brick, and blue and yellow tiling. All these schools are now listed and still open.

John Scott Health Centre
1952
London County Council Architect's Department
W.J. Durnford, A.E. Miller

The formation of the National Health Service in 1948 transferred the responsibility for healthcare in the capital away from the L.C.C. and onto the new organisation. However, the L.C.C. was still responsible for designing and building many healthcare related buildings, like clinics and ambulance stations. This was the first comprehensive health centre built in the country, created as part of the *Woodberry Down* estate just after WWII, and includes an adjoining nursery school. Designed very much in the prevailing postwar Scandinavian style, the health centre is built in brown and yellow brick with long ribbons of windows on its two floors. It was renamed in 1965 after John Scott, the L.C.C. Medical Officer of Health, and remains open to serve the public.

Battersea Ambulance Station
1960
London County Council Architect's Department

The early 1960s saw the expansion of the ambulance station
network in the capital, which like its fire stations were in need of
updating. The L.C.C. devised a standardised design able to be
adapted for a variety of sites. The design consists of a single
storey building, set in a square plan, with a garage area and
offices. The station is finished in white tiles, and features
bright blue folding doors. This station in Battersea replaced
an earlier station that had been destroyed in WWII. Other
examples of this version of ambulance station can still be found
in *Sutton*, *Tottenham*, *Mill Hill* and *Forest Hill*.

Hallfield School, Paddington
1953-54
Lindsay Drake and Denys Lasdun
Assisted by John Shaw

Two schools from the early postwar period proved to be
among the first steps in the storied careers of two famous
practises. Hallfield School was built as part of the Hallfield
estate in Paddington. Originally a project for Berthold Lubetkin
and Tecton, Denys Lasdun and Lindsay Drake took up the
scheme in 1948 when Tecton disbanded. The school was built
between 1953-54 for the L.C.C, with separate junior and infants
blocks. The buildings are set in the former grounds of large
Victorian houses, and the existing trees were preserved where
possible. The Junior School is formed of a curving two storey
block, with a striking glazed assembly hall. The infants block is
formed of four interconnected single storey classrooms. The
buildings are constructed with a concrete frame and brick infill,
and generous amounts of glazing. The screens to the roof water
tanks are made of translucent blue panels, adding colour to the
buildings palette.

Bousfield School, Kensington
1954-56
Chamberlin, Powell and Bon
Assisted by G.A. Agabeg, J. F. Connaughton,
R.K. Chisholm, M. Neylan

A little further west is Bousfield Primary, designed by
Chamberlin, Powell & Bon, known for their Golden Lane and
Barbican estates. Less ostentatiously brutal than Hallfield,
the building's palette is softened by the use of coloured
panels as part of the curtain walling. The entrance also
features a health and safety defying ornamental pond. The
concrete quotient is boosted by the spherical water tower
in the grounds, originally painted bright yellow. Chamberlin,
Powell & Bon also designed extensions to *Two Saints*
(now Ark Globe Academy) in Southwark, adding a pentagonal
hall block which has survived the school's redevelopment. A
significant surviving L.C.C. school of the same era is *Elliott
School* (1956) in Putney. Designed by G.A. Trevett and John
Bancroft, the new buildings brought together three separate
schools on the same site. The most eye-catching part of the
site is the curving, sculptural assembly hall.

Community Centre & Laundry, Parkview Estate, Bethnal Green
1953
De Metz & Birks

The bulk of the work of the L.C.C. in the immediate postwar years was the building of homes. Over one million homes had been destroyed or damaged during the Blitz, especially in east London. The L.C.C. and the Metropolitan Boroughs that made up London at the time, started a massive building programme from 1945, but were often beset by material and manpower shortages. The firm of De Metz & Birks designed the Parkview Estate in Bethnal Green for the L.C.C. The estate is built in the Festival style, with the most eye-catching building being the Community Centre and Laundry with its undulating curved roof. The first floor cantilevers out from the brick ground floor, and is fully glazed. The entrance also has a curved concrete canopy, balanced on thin iron poles.

Community Centre, Abbey Wood Estate, Greenwich
1959-64
London County Council Architect's Department

Another estate with an eye-catching community centre is
the Abbey Wood Estate on Eynsham Drive in Greenwich. Built
on land bought from the Woolwich Royal Arsenal munitions
factory, the estate centres around an 11-storey tower block.
Alongside it are a collection of community facilities; shops,
a health centre, library, a church and the community centre.
The centre has a star shaped roof, which rises in each corner,
allowing extra light into the hall. Aside from the tower block,
the housing consists of 3-storey blocks of maisonettes and
2-storey terraces and some bungalows. The area is in the
throes of redevelopment largely due to its place on the route
of the new Crossrail extension, with new homes being built left,
right and centre. Just behind the estate in Abbey Wood Park
is a piece of L.C.C. commissioned art, *"Delight"* (1962-67) by
A.H. Gerrard. It consists of a 27 ft long concrete frieze, with an
etched abstract pattern, depicting dancing figures (see back cover).

Jack Hobbs Club, Brandon Estate, Southwark
1958
London County Council Architect's Department
Edward Hollamby, D. Stamp, J.M. Macdonald,
E. Parsons, G.A. Knott, D.M. Gregory Jones,
A.P. Chapman, D.A. Woods

Edward Hollamby joined the L.C.C. in 1949, with his first job
being to design adjoining boys and girls secondary schools
in White City. He then moved to the Housing Division, and
oversaw the design of a number of estates until leaving for
Lambeth Borough in 1963. This guide focuses on the
non-housing work of the L.C.C., but here we have two
community buildings designed as part of estates by Hollamby
and his team. The Brandon Estate was built in Kennington
in the late 1950s. Alongside the point blocks and low rise
housing, the estate had a shopping centre, library and a
social club, as well as a sculpture by Henry Moore. The
Jack Hobbs Club was designed as the social centre for
the estate, and after a period of neglect has been refurbished
and reintegrated into the neighbourhood.

Youth Club, Pepys Estate, Deptford
1963
London County Council Architect's Department
Edward Hollamby, H.R.E. Knight, P.A. Westwood, D.M. Gregory Jones

Hollamby would also work on the Pepys Estate in Deptford, which was opened in 1966. It was built on the site of the Navy Victualling Yard, established in 1742. Phase one of the scheme saw 1500 homes built on the site, providing accommodation for 5000 people. As at the Brandon Estate, a variety of community amenities were provided, including a children's clinic, shopping centre, clubrooms, a day care centre and a youth club. This last building stands out due to its asymmetrical roofline, seemingly inspired by those of Kentish oast houses. Both estates have been through cycles of deterioration and redevelopment, with new buildings rising around the edges. Hollamby went on to work on the first plan of the Thamesmead estate before moving to Lambeth and developing some of the finest municipal housing estates of the 1960s and 70s.

The Lesson, Avebury Estate, Bethnal Green
1958
Franta Belsky

Sculpted Wall, Raglan Estate, Kentish Town
1965
Fred Millett

The L.C.C. and G.L.C. were major benefactors of modern art from 1946 onwards, commissioning thousands of pieces of artworks in various forms; murals, reliefs, sculptures, statues. Unfortunately much of this treasure trove of postwar art has been demolished, gone missing or been sold off. Work by Henry Moore, Barbara Hepworth, William Mitchell and many others is unaccounted for or in private hands. Some pieces have been listed and a few have been reinstated to their rightful places (or thereabouts). The L.C.C. held seven open air sculpture exhibitions in Battersea Park, then Holland Park, from 1948 until 1966, showcasing a wide range of approaches and materials.

An early example of the work commissioned by the L.C.C, is *"The Lesson"*, a sculpture in bronze of a mother helping a child to walk. It was designed by Franta Belsky, an artist from Czechoslovakia who left for Britain in 1939. Two casts were made of the statue, with one placed at the Avebury Estate and another at the *Rosa Bassett* (now Graveney) School in Tooting. Belsky also designed the *"Joyride"* sculpture overlooking Stevenage New Town centre.

More abstract work was commissioned, such as the sculpted wall installed as part of the *Raglan Estate* in Kentish Town. It was designed by Fred Millett, known for his murals and poster work. The wall (next page) consists of 10 small concrete monoliths, decorated with geometric reliefs and mosaic tiles, and was originally part of a playground, which has now been relocated. Works that have been protected include *"The Bull"* on the Alton Estate by Robert Clatworthy, David Wynee's *"Gorilla"* in Crystal Palace and Henry Moore's *"Two Piece Reclining Figure"* at the Brandon Estate, Southwark.

Ventilation Towers, Blackwall
1961-67
London County Council Architect's Department
Terry Farrell

The L.C.C. architect's department provided the starting point for many architects who went on to fame and fortune in the 1960s, 1970s, and beyond. Two projects brought two differing architects into the limelight. The Blackwall tunnel had opened in 1897 connecting the north and south sides of London. A second tunnel was added in the 1960s, necessitating additional ventilation. The Special Works Department under group leader Eric Hayes provided the distinctive curved concrete towers, designed by job architect Terry Farrell. Farrell went on to produce High Tech designs with Nicholas Grimshaw before becoming the PoMo king with his own practice, but here he produced a work of elegant brutalism. Formed of sprayed concrete over a reinforced steel frame, the towers are influenced by the work of Oscar Niemeyer in Brasilia. The northern vent can be seen between the buildings of Canary Wharf, and the southern one was incorporated into the Millennium Dome.

Michael Faraday Memorial, Elephant & Castle
1959-61
London County Council Architect's Department
Rodney Gordon

Another architect who got his start in the architect's department was Rodney Gordon, later the mastermind behind the brutalist output of the Owen Luder Partnership of the the 60s; The Tricorn Centre, Portsmouth, Eros House in Catford and Trinity Square, Gateshead. Here he designed an electricity substation that doubles as a memorial to scientist Michael Faraday. Instead of his signature concrete, we have a stainless steel box supported by an oversailing column and beam frame. Gordon's design originally had the box clad in glass revealing the inner workings of the transformer, but the fear of vandalism led the change to steel.

Roehampton Library, Alton Estate
1961
London County Council Architect's Department
John Partridge, Roy Stout

The Alton Estate in Roehampton was the L.C.C.'s flagship
estate of the immediate post war years. As well as showcasing
the forward looking direction of the departments housing
section, it neatly encapsulated the division between the older,
Scandinavian influenced faction and the younger group, led
by the future founders of Howell Killick Partridge & Amis,
leading the charge for the New Brutalism. The estate was built
between 1955-59, set on a sloping site on the edge of Richmond
Park. The estate library was added along with *Allbrook House*
in 1961, the work of John Partridge and Roy Stout. The library
building is single storey, and formed of a cluster of domes,
which brings in illumination via top lights. Both the library and
Allbrook House were denied listing in 2015 and their future is
in the balance.

School Dining & Assembly Hall, Brunswick Park School
1961-62
James Stirling & James Gowan
Assisted by Kenneth Davis

James Stirling and James Gowan met whilst working for Lyons
Ellis & Israel, later going into partnership with each other for a
brief but influential 7 years. One of their projects during this time was
an extension to Brunswick School in Camberwell Green, opposite
the L.C.C.'s own *Elmington Estate*. They added a new dining and
assembly hall to the Victorian school, as part of a larger rebuilding
project that was not realised. Three brick elevations rise from a
grass mound, their faces full glazed. They face west, south and east,
with the north quarter featuring a tall chimney. Inside the elevations
are supported by timber braces and rafters, with an exposed brick
finish. The pair also designed an old people's home for the L.C.C.
in 1964, *Perrygrove* in Charlton. The building was arranged in a
horseshoe plan, and built in their signature red brick. It has now
been demolished.

London College of Printing, Elephant & Castle
1962
Additions 1969-73
London County Council Architect's Department

London College of Fashion, Oxford Street
1963
London County Council Architect's Department
D. Rogers Stark, H.Blyth, G.Williams, A.Strutt, A.Thompson

As well as primary and secondary schools, the L.C.C. was responsible for Technical Colleges. Trade based places of education in London had flourished in the Victorian era, often as charitable foundations. In the 20th Century these came under the aegis of the L.C.C, and they sought to provide many of them with new premises during the postwar rebuilding boom. The *London College of Printing* had a new campus built at Elephant & Castle, overlooking the Rodney Gordon designed *Faraday Memorial*. The campus was formed of a 14 storey curtain wall tower block, with another 4 storey block alongside. Extensions were made from 1969, with studios and classrooms added featuring angled windows, allowing more natural light in. The institution became the London College of Communication in 1996, and the building is being redeveloped as part of the wider Elephant & Castle regeneration.

The London College of Fashion was formed from three trade schools for women, with the amalgamation of schools from Shoreditch, Clapham and Barrett Street (just off Oxford Street). The Barrett St school was rebuilt in 1962, to give a headquarters for the new establishment. The new building sits above shops by T.P. Bennett & Son, with a five storey structure made distinctive by a patterned grid of concrete and coloured glass. Behind this are more buildings, including a 22 storey office block. Like the London College of Communication, the College of Fashion became part of the University of Arts London in 2004. The College of Fashion will move to a new campus in the Olympic Park in 2023.

Woolwich Polytechnic
1959-64
London County Council Architect's Department
George Trevett, Ron Herron

After the confrontation of opposing styles at the *Alton Estate*, the brutalist influenced faction in the architects department held the upper hand. The Corbu influenced style predominated, particularly in the Education department under Michael Powell, head of the division from 1956, then I.L.E.A. chief from 1965-71. A number of new secondary schools, polytechnics and teaching colleges were built across the capital. These two buildings are good examples of the new, tough looking idiom, usually consisting of an exposed concrete frame with stock brick infill.

Woolwich Polytechnic had been founded in 1891, and expanded over 60 years into a jumble of Victorian era buildings with various extensions. A team from the Schools division under George Trevett and featuring future Archigram member Ron Herron, was tasked with providing a new extension, more in keeping with the era. The extension had to incorporate existing commercial buildings and face onto three different streets in central Woolwich with circulation between the blocks via the first floor and external bridges. The most interesting part is the l antern-like concrete lecture theatre on Thomas St, with its glazed mid-section.

The same New Brutalist style would also be used by private practises designing for the L.C.C. The Architects' Co-Partnership was formed in 1939 by a group of Architectural Association graduates, seeking to create a practice without hierarchy and dedicated to social renewal. They designed a collection of schools for the L.C.C., such as *Risinghill* in Islington (1960), run by progressive head Michael Duane. *The Beaufoy School* (later Lilian Baylis) was designed as part of a wider neighbourhood regeneration including the *Lambeth Walk* estate, also by the partnership. The school, now converted into private housing, shows the same brutalist hallmarks seen elsewhere; and exposed shuttered concrete frame, dark brick and glazed corridors. The school's plan consisted of linked teaching blocks with an octagonal hall, creating a series of asymmetrical courtyards. Like Woolwich Poly, circulation was via first floor galleries.

National Recreation Centre, Crystal Palace
1960-64
London County Council Architect's Department
Norman Engleback, E.R. Hayes, B.G. Jones,
M.J. Attenborough

In 1951 the L.C.C. were given the derelict site of the former exhibition centre at Sydenham. The site had housed the original Crystal Palace by Joseph Paxton, moved there from Hyde Park in 1852 and destroyed by fire in 1936. At first an exhibition centre was proposed to fill the site, before the counter idea of a National Sports Centre won out. The plan was developed by Leslie Martin, before Hubert Bennett took over in 1957, with Norman Engleback and E.R. Hayes as the project leaders.

Built between 1960 and 1964, the 200 acre site includes an athletics stadium plus a sports centre with swimming pools, squash courts and a boxing arena. The site also has housing for athletes, including an eleven storey hexagonal, timber covered tower block. The sports centre is the most prominent building, with its central concrete A-frame and fully glazed upper level. The building is entered on the upper floor by a walkway which sits above the grounds.

Inside, a forest of angled concrete columns support the roof, and forms a spine down the centre of the building. This structure allows the interior sports areas to be column free. The concrete theme is repeated in the pool area with a reinforced concrete diving platform at the north end. Nearby in the grounds is a corten steel bandstand, designed by Ian Ritchie in 1997 and nominated for the RIBA Stirling Prize.

Workshops, Adler Street, Whitechapel
1964
Yorke, Rosenberg & Mardall

Flatted Factories, Ada Street, Hackney
1966
Yorke, Rosenberg & Mardall

The redevelopment of the East End, with thousands of homes built to replace bomb damaged and substandard housing, changed the fabric of east London. The County of London Plan of 1943 recommended that industry be removed from built up neighbourhoods and relocated further out. However, some work spaces were to be situated in special zones to allow workers to live closer to their workplaces. This idea produced the flatted or unit factory, purpose built schemes containing workshops and offices.

The areas of Hackney and Tower Hamlets were deemed the most in need of the flatted factory, with the firm of Yorke, Rosenberg and Mardall given the commission to build a number of them. Some have been redeveloped, but the two most prominent survivors are those in Adler Street, Whitechapel and Ada Street, Hackney.

Adler Street is a five storey scheme containing 15 workshops, as well as ground floor shops. The building is constructed of reinforced concrete with infill panels of grey brick. The Ada Street (left) scheme is larger, with an 8 storey building that allowed the small business occupiers to use shared heavy goods lifts and storage facilities. It is now a work/studio space for the creatives of Hackney.

Shoreditch Fire Station
1965
London County Council Architect's Department
A.R. Borrett, T.M. Williams

The L.C.C. designed and built a swathe of Arts and Crafts
inspired fire stations between 1890 and 1910. By the 1960s,
these buildings were deemed to be in need of replacement,
and a new set of stations were built all around the capital.
The Special Works Department, under Geoffrey Horsfall,
was responsible for the design of the new stations. They used
the brutalist vernacular of the day, with exposed concrete
frames, brick infill and cantilevered windows. All these elements
can be seen at Shoreditch Fire Station on Old Street. The
station includes four staff maisonettes complete with private
patios, and has a reinforced concrete drill tower at the rear.

Chelsea Fire Station
1965
London County Council Architect's Department
*D. Rogers Stark, R. Robson Smith. M.G. Booth,
Warren Chalk*

A new fire station on the Kings Road in Chelsea was also
built, opening in March 1965. This one had been planned from
the late 1950s, with Warren Chalk involved in the process. As
well as a fire station, an adjoining *College of Art* and student
accommodation was also built. The fire station is more Pop Art
than Brutalist, with its sans serif black station sign on the
white facade and bright red fire doors. The now demolished
college building to the rear was clad in white mosaic slabs
and had continuous window strips and pyramid roof lights to
bring in illumination to the teaching studios. Stations were also
built at Clapham and Lewisham in the same period. *Clapham*
(1962-4) is a four storey building with generous glazing built
to replace a station from 1863. *Lewisham* (1967) is more like
Shoreditch, with a grid-like facade in dark brick and an exposed
staircase.

Mural, Islington Green School
1965
William Mitchell

Tower Building, North Western Polytechnic
1966
G.L.C. Department of Architecture and Civic Design

The sculptor William Mitchell joined the L.C.C. in the 1950s,
after some time in the Royal Navy and also studying at the Royal
College of Art and in Italy. His job at the L.C.C. was to produce
decorative artworks for the many housing projects put up by the
architect's department in the postwar period. Examples of his
work can be seen at estates such as *Derby Hill* in Lewisham and
the *Winstanley Estate* in Battersea. After establishing his own
practice in the early 1960s, Mitchell still produced work for the
L.C.C. His mural (next page) for the now demolished *Islington
Green School* by Scherrer & Hicks, is somewhat atypical of
Mitchell's work, with a mosaic of multi-coloured geometric
patterned circles instead of the usual concrete forms. The
mural was one of a pair at the site, the other being demolished
when the school was rebuilt.

William Mitchell also produced a long exterior concrete relief
for the new buildings on Holloway Road built as part of the
North Western Polytechnic's 1960s expansion. The mural was
demolished in 2000 for Daniel Libeskind's new Graduate Centre.
The 15-storey Tower Building (left) is an energetic brutalist design,
with a bold concrete structure and horizontal window bands which
turn around each corner of the building. North Western opened
in 1929 and by the time the Tower Building was completed was
the largest Polytechnic in London. It merged with the Northern
Polytechnic in 1971 to become the Polytechnic of North London
before turning into a University in 1992.

Queen Elizabeth Hall, Purcell Room & Hayward Gallery 1963-8
G.L.C. Department of Architecture and Civic Design
Jack Whittle, Geoffrey Horsfall, W. J. Appleton, E.J. Blyth, Norman Engleback, J.W. Szymaniak

The Festival of Britain site was cleared, bar the Festival Hall, after the event had finished, leaving a gap on the South Bank to be filled. A combined concert hall, performance space and art gallery would provide a new cultural centre alongside the extended Festival Hall. The new complex was planned from 1958, with future members of Archigram; Warren Chalk, Ron Herron and Dennis Crompton, under the leadership of Norman Engleback, responsible for the designs. Their plans included an opera house, national theatre (later realised by Denys Lasdun), conference centre and hotel. The Archigrammers left the L.C.C. before it became the G.L.C., with Englenback and E.J. Blyth leading the project to completion.

The Queen Elizabeth Hall and Purcell Room opened on 1st March 1967, able to accommodate over 1400 people between them, with the Hayward Gallery opening in July 1968. The finished scheme is boldly Brutalist, a retort to the comparatively placid Festival Hall next door (even with its extensions). The concrete structure is a mixture of prefabricated and in situ elements 15 inches thick for sound insulation, with Cornish granite infill panels. Externally, the complex presents itself as a series of blocks and walkways, somewhat confusing from afar but with its own logic close up.

Various plans and schemes have been made to alter or even demolish the complex. Richard Rogers proposed covering the site with a glass roof in the 90s, and the famous skatepark undercroft was due to be turned into a retail area, until the plans were dropped after a widely supported campaign against them. The whole riverside area, including the R.F.H. and the National Theatre has become a popular public space, with the three refurbished G.L.C. buildings part of the scenery.

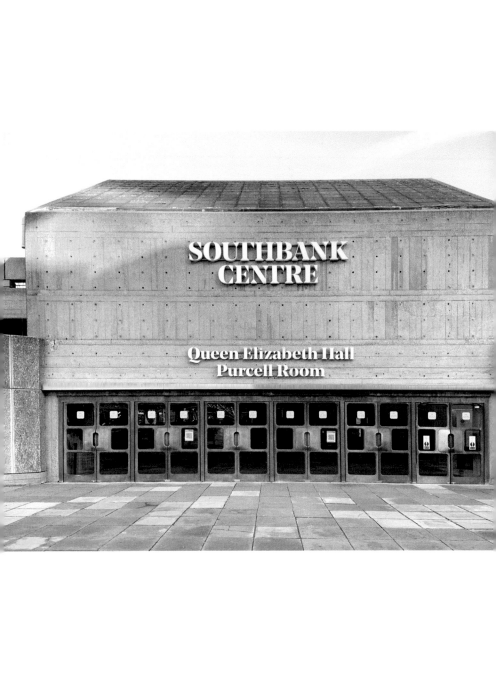

Haggerston School for Girls, Hackney
1964-67
Erno Goldfinger & Associates
Assisted by L. Nowicki. J. Blacker, N. Molis

Acland Burghley School, Camden
1963-67
Howell, Killick, Partridge & Amis

The L.C.C. was one of the first local authorities in the country to adopt the Comprehensive model for secondary education, allowing universal secondary education for 11-15 year olds. This necessitated the building of new, modern school buildings all over the capital. The boom in demand on the architect's department school group, led by Michel Powell, was eased by the use of private practices to produce new designs.

Many other now-famous names were bought in to design new schools. Erno Goldfinger, who had previously designed two primary schools for the L.C.C, was commissioned to produce a girls school at Haggerston in Hackney. His plan had three linked blocks, including classrooms, an assembly hall, a gymnasium and a library. The building is constructed in a typically tough Goldfinger style, with a reinforced concrete frame and blue brick infill. Both the school buildings and the cuboid caretakers house are Grade II listed. Two of Goldfinger's most famous later works, *Trellick* and *Balfron* towers, would be designed for G.L.C. estates in the 1960s.

Another practice who had previous experience with the L.C.C. were Howell, Killick, Partridge & Amis, whose founders had been part of the *Alton Estate* design team. They were given the job for a new secondary school in Tufnell Park, Camden, bringing a boys and girls school together. The small site was extended over the adjacent railway line by building a concrete deck to accommodate the playground and sports hall. The main school building is formed of a 3-storey admin block, with three 5-storey teaching blocks branching off. The buildings are all formed of reinforced concrete with aggregate concrete infill panels. Like Haggerston, Acland Burghley is now Grade II listed.

The most famous L.C.C./G.L.C. school was *Pimlico Secondary*, designed by John Bancroft, and built between 1965-70. Described by one critic as a "battleship", the glass and concrete structure housed 1,725 pupils in its sunken plot, and featured an automated glazing system. Unfortunately this system was imperfect, leading to a hot building in summer and a cold one in winter. Like many schools of its era, it succumbed to New Labour's Building Schools for the Future programme and was demolished in 2008.

College of Architecture and Advanced Building Technology, Marylebone Road
1966-70
G.L.C. Department of Architecture and Civic Design
Michael Powell, Alan Strutt, Ron Ringshall, Frank Kinder, J. Buckrell

College of Engineering and Science, New Cavendish Street
1966-70
Lyons, Israel & Ellis
Tom Ellis, R. Simpson, J. McCain, R. MacCormac, M.Blank, J.Cannon

The Royal Polytechnic Institution opened on Regent Street in 1838, the first Polytechnic in London, allowing higher education for all. By 1960 the Poly was under the control of the L.C.C., who added two new colleges, in order to expand and update the courses available.Two new campuses were built, one on the Marylebone Road for Architecture and Advanced Building Technology (C.A.A.B.T.), and another on New Cavendish Street for Engineering and Science (C.E.S.). The C.A.A.B.T. campus was designed by the L.C.C. architect's department just before the G.L.C. came into being. The main range faces boldly on to the Marylebone Road, with an overhanging top floor. Behind are more buildings, again in painted concrete, with a pronounced horizontal emphasis. Two thin towers complete the site, one for student accommodation, the other for social tenants.

At the same time as the Marylebone Campus was being constructed, the College of Engineering and Science was also being built, a 15 minute walk away on New Cavendish St. This campus was designed by the firm of Lyons, Israel & Ellis, prominent for their tough brutalist designs such as the National Theatre Studios and the Wolfson Institute in Hammersmith. The L.I.& E. campus balances reinforced concrete construction with bronze coloured curtain walled glass and a cantilevered lecture hall on the street facade. The polytechnic is nowadays part of the University of Westminster.

Pedestrian Footbridges, Thamesmead Estate
1967-1973
G.L.C. Department of Architecture and Civic Design

Overall architectural team included: J.G.H.D. Cairns, Geoffrey Horsfall, Robert Rigg, Phillip Bottomley, Norman Engleback, J.A. Roberts, John Knight, G.A. Comrie-Smith, P.A. Westwood & others

A large estate had been planned on the marshes of Plumstead and Erith from the early 1960s. It was intended to be a mini-city accommodating 60,000 people, with a combination of buildings for housing, work and leisure facilities. Architect Robert Rigg drew up the master plan for the estate. Inspired by Swedish planning ideas, he spread the housing around waterways and lakes connected by a system of walkways, hoping to produce a calm and serene atmosphere. The original plan was never finished, with the tide turning against the creation of megastructures and large estates in the 1970s, leading to a scaled down version of the future.

The first phase of housing was arranged with tower blocks and long, snaking ranges of maisonettes connected by pedestrian walkways. Aside from housing, a range of buildings and structures serving other functions were designed. The most spectacular was the *Health Centre* (1972) designed by Derek Stow & Partners, which hovered above the central lake on steel piers, now demolished. On the north side of the lake is the *Boat Club* (1980), designed by the G.L.C. Parks Department. Now called the Lakeside Centre, it has undergone renovation and rebranding. The G.L.C. also built *The Moorings Community Centre* (1976) and *Hawksmoor Youth Club* (1977), both designs reflective of the turn away from concrete towards brick, timber and tile as the 1970s wore on. The most interesting of the schools built for the area is *Waterfield* (1975). Looking more like an industrial unit by Nicholas Grimshaw or Norman Foster than a school, it has been altered somewhat and is now called Woolwich Polytechnic School.

The estate is now being redeveloped by Peabody, with much of the original 1960s design demolished. One part that still exists for now is the Pedestrian Footbridge (1973, next page) to the north of the first phase, a mini suspension bridge with sculptural concrete A-frames hovering above Eastern Way, a reminder of the intricate network of pathways and pedestrian bridges built into the estate.

Vittoria School, Islington
1968
Inner London Education Authority
G.L.C. Department of Architecture and Civic Design
R. Robson Smith

Bromley Hall School
1968
Inner London Education Authority
G.L.C. Department of Architecture and Civic Design
Bob Giles

Control of education was reorganised when the G.L.C. came into being in 1965.
In the suburbs, responsibility for education was given to the newly created boroughs.
In inner London, education came under the control of the new Inner London Education
Authority (I.L.E.A.), which also became responsible for designing schools. Vittoria
School carried on from *Eveline Lowe School* in Camberwell (1967), in having a plan
that separated classrooms via pavilions and a versatile interior layout. The school
buildings are built in brick and timber boarding, with a steel framed assembly hall.
Also in Islington is *Hugh Myddelton School* by Julian Sofaer, a sturdy design in brown
brick and timber fascia board. *Benthal Primary* (1967) in Hackney took a different
approach. Designed by Paul Maas, the school features 8 pavilions with the appearance
of large tents, each a self contained hub for a class group. The school was nearly
demolished in 2018 when Hackney Council looked to reorganise its school facilities,
luckily the plan was scrapped.

The L.C.C. and G.L.C. also designed a number of schools for those with greater
needs than available through mainstream education of the period. Buildings were
specially designed to improve the learning environment of those with physical
challenges. For instance, the *Frank Barnes School for Deaf Children* in Camden,
designed by Ivor Plummer, featured concrete block walls to dampen noise and
vibrations from a nearby road. Others like *Ickburgh* in Hackney by Norman Foster
& Partners used an open plan, designed to remove mobility barriers. Bromley Hall
School (left) in Poplar was designed by Bob Giles to cater for pupils between 5 and
16, with a range of disabilities. It is sited next to the Blackwall Tunnel Approach road,
and as at Frank Barnes school, the design shields the pupils from noise, with a
scheme that has a group of pavilion classrooms surrounded by a high brick wall.
The classrooms are illuminated by top lights in the pyramid roofs of each structure.
The school closed in 2002, and it sits rather forlornly waiting for a new purpose.

George Green's School was originally founded in 1828, by shipbuilder George Green
on the East India Dock Road. The need for expansion saw it move to Manchester
Road on the Isle of Dogs in the 1970s. The rebuild provided a number of other
community buildings: a youth club, an old people's day centre, an adult education
institute and a nursery. The design of the school is reminiscent of the Alexandra Road
Estate in Camden by Neave Brown, with three long stepped blocks facing towards the
Thames. They are built in concrete blockwork around an exposed concrete frame,
originally with steel windows, now largely replaced. Extensions have been made to the
school to allow for extra teaching space, but this has not detracted from the original
design.

Vittoria School, Islington

Benthal Primary School, Hackney

Hugh Myddelton School, Islington

George Green's School, Isle of Dogs

Bethnal Green Fire Station
1969
G.L.C. Department of Architecture and Civic Design

Paddington Fire Station
1969
G.L.C. Department of Architecture and Civic Design
B.H.S Thaxton, R.Bix. J. Knight, Max Brewer

After the new fire stations of the mid-1950s and 1960s, came
another wave at the end of the latter decade. New stations were
built all around the capital, with a number in east London. The
most interesting architecturally was the new station at Bethnal
Green, on Roman Road. It integrates fire fighting facilities with
adjacent flats, all in dark brick with an exposed concrete frame.
Nearby, new stations were built at *Poplar* (1970), *Homerton* (1972),
Stoke Newington (1974), and *Kingsland* (1975). The latter three
stations were all built in a similar single-storey style

In the west, *Paddington Fire Station* was opened the same year.
Its design is unusual amongst fire stations of its time in taking the
form of an inverted ziggurat, with an overhanging top floor. Of
course this form was used elsewhere in the era, most notably at
John Madin's now demolished Birmingham Central Library. The
rear practice yard features a drill tower made up of prefabricated
concrete sections. It is one of the busiest stations in London,
with over 2000 call outs every year. Other new fire stations of
the time included *Bexley* (1969), *Silvertown* (1969) *Kentish Town*
(1972) and *Holloway* (1975). The first three are alike in design,
with a two-storey brick building with exterior metal cladding.

Just as the G.L.C. continued to upgrade Fire Stations in the late 1960s and 70s, they also did the same with Ambulance Stations. The Special Works Department moved on from the tiled, white box used across various sites in the early 1960s, towards individual designs. A new headquarters and station for London Ambulance was built on Lambeth Road in 1973. A more adventurous design was used for the station at *Bromley* (right). Set amid suburban terraces, the red engineering brick structure has no windows, with light admitted to the interior via the space frame roof of metal and glass.

Camden Ambulance Station on Cressy Road, uses a similar palette of materials, red brick and glass, with an angled arrangement. The offices are arranged in a polygonal plan stepping upwards, with the garage to one side and a service area with an overhanging blue space frame canopy (now removed). Other ambulance stations of note include *North Kensington* (1968), built underneath the Western Avenue extension flyover and *Woolwich* (1970), included as part of a complex with a store and repair room for the Woolwich Ferry service.

Bromley Ambulance Station
1972
G.L.C. Department of Architecture and Civic Design
Henry White, Bernard Binsted, Ian Napier, R. Bonsal, M. Racheter

Camden Ambulance Station
1975
G.L.C. Department of Architecture and Civic Design
Henry White, Derek Wells

Waltham Forest Magistrates Court
1973
G.L.C. Department of Architecture and Civic Design
Jake Brown, Noel Cowburn, J.H. Newman

Inner London Sessions Courthouse
1974
G.L.C. Department of Architecture and Civic Design
F.O. Brown, R. Davis

Richmond Magistrates Court
1975
G.L.C. Department of Architecture and Civic Design
E.J. Blyth, M.Brewer

In 1969 the G.L.C. produced a report setting out guidelines for building new courts in the London region. The authority had taken on responsibility for overseeing legal buildings in the capital after the switch from the L.C.C. in 1965. A number of new magistrates courts were built around the capital, particularly in the suburbs, in the 1970s. The first to be opened was at Walthamstow with a design developed by Jake Brown and Noel Cowburn. The long, low structure fits into the existing landscape which includes the 1930s civic centre by P.D. Hepworth. It is built in reinforced concrete and faced with Portland stone, like its neighbour. The building contains court rooms, offices, waiting rooms and holding cells. The courthouse is currently scheduled for demolition.

Further court facilities were built at *Redbridge*, *Richmond* and *Bexley*. The building at Richmond is planned in a similar way to Waltham Forest, with separated facilities for defendants, witnesses and lawyers, and a mixture of different sized courtrooms. The building lays under the flightpath for Heathrow and had to be suitably insulated to allow proceedings to be heard properly. The courthouse was closed in 2016 and threatened with demolition, but was given a pardon and converted into offices. The 1921 *Inner London Sessions Courthouse* in Southwark was also extended in a suitably 1970s style, with a steel and smoked glass structure on Avonmouth Street.

Inner London Sessions Courthouse

nond Magistrates Court

School of Communication, Riding House Street
1976
Lyons Israel Ellis & Gray
Tom Ellis, C.J. Stevens, J. Roberts, R. Maers, D. Triggs,
J. Ellis, C.Ellis, J. Cannon

Expansion of the further education network in London was
undertaken by the G.L.C. throughout the 1970s. Lyons Israel
Ellis & Gray, who had designed the New Cavendish Street
campus for the Polytechnic of London, added a concrete and
glass tower extension and studios for television and cinema
to the 1929 building in Riding House Street by F.J. Willis.
Despite towering above the streetscape, the staircase tower
is fairly inconspicuous, and nods towards the High Tech idiom
with its exposed service pipes seen through the glass. Lyons
Israel Ellis & Gray drew up plans for further expansion of the
building towards Great Portland Street, but these were not
used.

Hammersmith and West London College
1980
Inner London Education Authority
G.L.C. Department of Architecture and Civic Design
Bob Giles

A larger project was completed further west in Hammersmith
on the site of St. Paul's school which moved in 1969. The
plan is formed of linked crescent-shaped blocks, designed
to shield the inhabitants from the traffic noise of the
neighbouring A4. A piazza-style open space sits in the centre
of the blocks, allowing a quiet area for breaks and socialising.
The buildings are constructed of the favoured red engineering
brick of the era, hiding the in-situ concrete frame. The red brick
is also used for the building steps, walls and external paving.
The all-encompassing red is relieved in part by the projecting
black window frames that run around the building. The campus
is now part of Ealing, Hammersmith and West London College,
and the building has been earmarked by the college for
redevelopment into a mixed used scheme.

Thames Barrier
1984
Rendell, Palmer & Tritton
G.L.C Department of Architecture and Civic Design
B.H.S. Thaxton, Alan Stockley, Dick Richardson, Anil Kapse,
Alan Eyles, Jean Clapham, Tony Petty, Alan Gardener,
Dhiraj Dudhia

Now a much beloved symbol of safety and ingenuity, the Thames
Barrier was seen in its planning stages by some as a vanity project
by the G.L.C. Its building was prompted by the 1953 North Sea
flood, which made over 200 people homeless along the length of
the estuary. After various investigations were held,building began
in 1974 with a consortium of construction companies responsible
for the build. The ingenious design for the rotating cylinder barriers
was devised by Charles Draper, with engineering by Rendell,
Palmer & Tritton. The 520 metre wide barrier is formed of 10 gates
connected by 9 concrete piers, overlooked by a control tower.
The G.L.C architects department were responsible for the steel
roof shells which have become an iconic part of London's river
landscape. As well as the control tower with its inverted roofline,
the architect's department also designed a shoreside restaurant,
cafe and visitors centre, in typically 1980s style with glass, steel
and plastic cladding.

East Greenwich Fire Station
1985
G.L.C Department of Architecture and Civic Design
Jack Lambert, Peter Smith

North Kensington Fire Station
1985
G.L.C Department of Architecture and Civic Design
Dhiraj Dudhia

Fire Command Centre, Albert Embankment
1985
G.L.C Department of Architecture and Civic Design
Vincent Pilato

Some of the last completed projects by the G.L.C. Architects
Department were updated facilities for the London Fire Brigade.
A new *Command and Mobilising Centre* was built at the rear of
the L.F.B. headquarters on Albert Embankment. Replacing three
regional centres with one computer aided control facility, the
building was designed by Vincent Pilato with a combination of
steel and brick. A steel frame is infilled with dark brick, and steel
panels finish the overhanging second floor and top floor pod.
The brigade moved their HQ to Southwark in 2008, and have
tried to redevelop the site with the demolition of the Command
centre. For now, the proposals have been rejected.

A number of new fire stations were also built at the same time,
eschewing the concrete of previous decades in favour of
something more colourful and contemporary. *North Kensington*
uses a High Tech palette of a bright red steel frame and metal
cladding, with the 1982 new style steel drill tower in the rear yard.
This design, by Jake Brown, David Cook and Vincent Pilato,
replaces the previous brick or concrete tower structure with
prefabricated steel sections, assembled on site. *East Greenwich*
(left), also opened in 1985, is constructed in steel and brick infill,
with curved bays and a bright red finish.

References & Further Reading

Trevor Dannatt- Modern Architecture in Britain *Batsford 1959*

Royston Landau- New Directions in British Architecture *Studio Vista 1968*

Michael Webb- Architecture in Britain Today *Country Life 1969*

G.L.C. Architecture 1956-70 *G.L.C. 1970*

Robert Maxwell- New British Architecture *Thames & Hudson 1972*

Eugene Rosenberg- Architect's Choice: Art in Architecture in Great Britain since 1945 *Thames & Hudson 1982*

G.L.C./I.L.E.A. Architecture 1976-1986 *Architectural Press 1986*

Bridget Cherry, Charles O'Brien & Nikolaus Pevsner Buildings of England London 2: South *Yale University Press 2002*

Bridget Cherry, Charles O'Brien & Nikolaus Pevsner- Buildings of England London 5: East *Yale University Press 2004*

Geriant Franklin, Elain Harwod, Simon Taylor & Matthew Whitfield- England's Schools 1962-88 A Thematic Study *English Heritage 2012*

Ruth Lang- Architects Take Command *Volume #41 2014*

The Archigram Archival Project Website